City Of Lost Memories

TOLU' A. AKINYEMI

First published in Great Britain as a
softback original in 2022

Copyright © Tolu' A. Akinyemi
The moral right of the author has been asserted.
All rights reserved.

No part of this publication may be reproduced, stored in a retrieval system, or transmitted, in any form or by any means, without the prior permission in writing of the author, nor be otherwise circulated in any form of binding or cover other than that in which it is published and without a similar condition including this condition being imposed on the subsequent purchaser.

Cover Design: Buzz Designz

Published by 'The Roaring Lion Newcastle'
ISBN: 978-1-913636-32-6
eISBN: 978-1-913636-33-3

Email:
tolu@toluakinyemi.com
author@tolutoludo.com

Website:
www.toluakinyemi.com
www.tolutoludo.com

ALSO, BY Tolu' A. Akinyemi from
The Roaring Lion Newcastle'

"Dead Lions Don't Roar" (A collection of Poetic Wisdom for the Discerning Series 1)
"Unravel your Hidden Gems" (A collection of Inspirational and Motivational Essays)
"Dead Dogs Don't Bark" (A collection of Poetic Wisdom for the Discerning Series 2)
"Dead Cats Don't Meow" (A collection of Poetic Wisdom for the Discerning Series 3)
"Never Play Games with the Devil" (A collection of Poems)
"A Booktiful Love" (A collection of Poems)
"Inferno of Silence" (A collection of Short Stories)
"Black ≠ Inferior" (A collection of Poems)
"Never Marry A Writer" (A collection of Poems)
"Everybody Don Kolomental" (A collection of Poems)
"I Wear Self-Confidence Like a Second Skin" (Children's Literature)
"I am Not a Troublemaker" (Children's Literature)
"Born in Lockdown" (A collection of Poems)
"A god in a Human Body" (A collection of Poems)
"If You Have To Be Anything, Be Kind" (Children's Literature)

Dedication

To my charmazing partner, Olabisi,
thank you for the booktiful memories.

Acknowledgements

A big thank you to the editors of the journals below, for giving my poems their first abode.

'Heaven Help' first appeared in Agape Review.

'At Rest With the Sea' first appeared in Calla Press.

'Grandfather's Face' first appeared in My Woven Poetry.

All the glory goes to the Lord for the grace, infinite mercies, and ability to write my sixteenth published work. I'm super thankful.

To my booktiful family, Olabisi, Isaac and Abigail, sincere appreciation for the love and support on the home front. I love you now and always!

Special thanks to my wonderful parents, Gabriel and Temidayo Akinyemi, for the love and support through the years.

Huge appreciation to Adeola Gbalajobi and Diane Donovan for editing and proofreading this collection.

A final thanks to everyone who has supported me on this journey that keeps unravelling so many booktiful experiences.

Contents

Don't 2
Romantic Agony 3
Grandfather's Face 4
Refurbished Democrat 5
Letters From the Past 6
Daemon Forest 7
Men Are Scarce 8
This Generation 9
Poetic Frame 10
Memory Lane.. 11
Innocence... 12
Survival Mode 13
Love Like Crimson 14
Remembrance 15
Anger 16
Drowning 17
Celebration... 18
Figure of Speech... 19
Sweet Nothings... 20
Fake Love... 21
Burning Memories.. 22
Memoriam of History 23

Malice	24
History	25
Blurt Out	26
Heartfelt Prayer	27
Help Heaven	28
At Rest With the Sea	29
Chronicles On the Seafront	30
Blur	31
Colonial Masters	32
Creative God	33
Blurred	34
City of Lost Memories	35
Entitled Uncle	36
At the Table	37
Never Ever!	38
On Loss	40
Needy	41
Addiction	43
Fizzling	44
Author's Note	45
Author's Bio	47

City of Lost Memories

POEMS

Don't

Don't wash me away from your memory.
Your knowledge of me should be immersed
in profundities,
not faded like an eroded land.

Don't colour me in dark paints
like a victim of contorted history…
My affinity with kindness
should not be wiped in a haze.

Don't wish your evil plans upon me.
My snow-white innocence
is a shield to guard me from looming danger.

Romantic Agony

My ex is carrying my seed to the grave
Words spoken in anger are haunting

Her eyes were a dam of salty water
My tears were sorrow-laden like a vessel
dripping oil

I grieve for what could have been
and our children, who never live beyond our
fantasies.

Grandfather's Face

My grandfather's face has been swallowed by the fog;
his memories, a fading paint on an old wall.

Time has eroded every treasured moment;
his stories are now a forgotten song.

Refurbished Democrat

Eight years have been wasted by the presidential aspirant
who knocked on the door with relentless fervour
and harvested perennial losses.

He posed himself as the nation's Messiah;
shed impassioned tears
until he was whitewashed by propagandists.

He has soiled the sacred office with nepotism and tribalism.
The nation sank in poverty.
The anti-corruption hero is a whitewashed coffin.

He is desperate for a legacy—
he would have it
that memories of a regime filled with pain, suffering, and agony
won't be rewritten by revisionists who will clothe the devil
in the garment of the Messiah.

Letters From the Past

The letters from the past are haunting,
the morning cloud is heavy with agony
and the night echoes horror.

Let humanity rain kindness on us,
that our fragility will be a remembrance of brokenness
and the letters from the past will spur a new narrative
that will erase these chilling woes.

Daemon Forest

The evil forest house daemons, with unusual body shapes.
This forest echoes with woe.

Our chemistry with the past gleams with pain,
an evil narrative with power-hungry gods as the characters.

The evil forest is a melting pot of unholy alliance,
a marriage of bitter rivals.

Let this alliance perish.
Let this unholy matrimony die a natural death,
that men may enjoy the air of freedom.

Men Are Scarce

Will God come from heaven to help the helpless?
For good men are scarce, like precious gems.

The anthem of ingrates
reeks of disdain and
a truckload of complaints.

This Generation

This generation is plagued by forgetfulness.
The past has been crucified on the cross of hypocrisy.

This generation of entitled children are fanning
the embers of hate.
We have forgotten how to take lessons from the past.

Poetic Frame

My poetic frame is gigantic
but it's being downplayed by familiar spirits.

My poetic fame is spreading like gossips
but it's being undermined by failed dreamers.

My literary statue is built on solid ground,
standing tall like twin towers - it's here to stay 'till the end of time.

Memory Lane

I take a walk back in time to those days
when the future was in peril.
I soak in the hopelessness
of nights when hope was thin and
unreachable.
To remember the past is to keep life in
perspective,
a walk down memory lane keeps the future
in focus.

Innocence

Life begins in innocence.
The heart of a child is an unsoiled field
until the knowledge of the world corrupts it.

Midlife crisis is the lot of many:
days of relentless struggles and
the rediscovery of one's self.

The end of life is a journey back to
innocence,
the waning of the memory, and a
longing to take off the earthly coat.

Survival Mode

The poor are pawns in the hands of the rich,
like legos in the hands of a child.

The poor are teaching the rich
the value of savings—
a paradox that surprises me.

The poor are pandering to the rich,
selling their souls for crumbs and handouts;
sacrificing their pride on the altar of survival.

Love Like Crimson

The heart of man is a cloud heavy with hate;
his tongue, a nest of evil.

Deep clean this heart with hyssop and holy water;
erase past memories, along with its aches.

Remembrance

Your pretence is a stench in the air.
Your words take the shape of an arrow.

Your memory floods my heart with sorrow.
It leaves me with the taste of a bad dream.

Anger

His anger is a wrecking ball
breaking family bonds.
His emotions are a broken dam.
The anger raging like a burning furnace
is a sign of impending ruin.

Drowning

I drown my fears with spirits and forget my
sorrows - momentarily
before they re-emerge from the rack of my
mind.
I drown my tears in the ocean of hope before
I tire from weariness.

My ego isn't bloated, like my rising fame.
I paper the cracks over my weakness
as a sign of youthful vigour.

The voices in my head ring hollow.
I wear despair like a second skin.

Celebration

Our murmuring is a recurring tune.
The narrative of vengeance spreads its wings.

The morning dew has been tainted by a gleam of sorrow.
Our banquet of celebration has been overshadowed by pangs of regret.

My neighbor was swallowed in the ocean of worries.

How do you feast when sorrow fouls the air?
How do you eat when many stomachs ache and rumble from emptiness?

How do you celebrate without an axe to grind?

Figure of Speech

Atropos is dying slowly.
He spends his days squirming
and the nights in a duel with unseen
demons.

Atropos is a metaphor—

his whole life has been lived in the shadows;
his memory is a dying flame.

Sweet Nothings

I planted butterflies in her belly with words,
Sweet nothings that set her heart aflame
with passion,
Empty.

Today, I am a surgeon of love
Piecing together fragments of a broken heart.

Fake Love

He wrote an elegy for the love he lost;
an epistle for the void in his heart.
He inked flowery words for likes
and virtual consolation.

Why paint a picture of love where hate
reigns?
How do you grieve from a place of
emptiness?
Why soil the memory of the dead with your
~~fake~~ love?

My heart is not a place to break into and out
of.

My ~~fake~~ friends are looking for me.
My tap of favour never runs dry,
but I no longer lie in bed with strange
fellows—

They repulse me like the aftermath of a
hangover.
I no longer feel emotions for friends
that ghost in and out of my life like a
revolving door.

Burning Memories

When he is raging,
he is burning
memories that took years to build.
I no longer give advice to the hard-hearted.

Why waste words on the hot-headed?

I once told a young man to have a cool head.
He didn't respond with atrocious rage at my insanity.
What he did afterwards remains shrouded in mystery.

Maybe he was cussing, vexing, or took it with a pinch—
only time will tell.

I have learnt to treasure silent walls, the stillness of nights,
and being labelled a man of few words.

Memoriam of History

The wall of remembrance has been crushed.

We walk in the nakedness
of unbridled ignorance.
Overbloated egos are an obstruction.

I'm a voice of reason.
I came to the party some decades late.

My name has been watermarked
in the memoriam of history.
This watershed moment is causing a ruckus.

Malice

Hate is like termites; it eats the heart like wood.
Hate is a veil that clouds sound judgement.

It doesn't take the world to wear humility on your sleeve.
My head is an amalgamation of ideas,
Of thoughts, of dreams, of visions, of the weight of the world.

I carry destiny on sturdy shoulders.

History

Pain and hurt lie in the pages of the past
And history breeds regrets.
A dive into it opens fresh wounds

Blurt Out

Blurt out this pain that holds you by the
larynx
and makes you a shadow.
Your corrosive nature
is a ticking bomb.

Shed this baggage
that has left you on the brink of demise.

Exhume this hurt
that wears you thin and pushes you closer to
doomsday.

Heartfelt Prayer

The guilt of sin haunts my soul.

I can't see the ark
Or the rainbow.

Life's darts and arrows are piercing me,
But the stream of healing is dry.
This burden of fear weighs me down,
I can't raise my head to see the sunshine of hope.
I say a soft prayer, and
my heart knocks on heaven's door

Bathe me in agape love, I pray.
Wipe away the sins that blemish my soul
Save me from the throes of evil,
This weight of guilt
That overwhelms me.

Help Heaven

Heaven helps those without pride and ego.
Heaven helps the
Meek
And gives strength to the weak.

Help heaven to rain cloud of mercies
To wash away your worries.
God never fails; He is never late.
Help heaven steer the course of your
anguished soul
And grant you rest.

At Rest With the Sea

At sea, tranquillity spreads like God's eyes
upon the earth.
Nature is a miracle;
the songs of the birds and the ducks
that colour the surface of the sea.

Nature is spreading its wings.
The blue sky is a silent melody.

A poet's lens is on autofocus
to capture the magic of nature.

Chronicles On the Seafront

I saw a cruise ship today and
I imagine myself touring the world.

By God, I fear large waters, but at the moment,
I'd join the ship and tour the world, leaving my cares behind.

Like Jesus,
My spirit detests gambling.

I have a few delusional friends
Who dream of winning the lottery.

Part-time gambling isn't an occupation.
Addiction is a curse.

Wean yourself of the urge
With the prescription of honesty.

On the seafront, my weakness is unravelled
before my naked Eyes.

Blur

Yesterday's milk of kindness is today a sour grape.

Yesterday's destiny helper is now a subject of scorn—
Forget his good deeds and develop amnesia to his kindness.

Is memory a thing without shape?
Is remembrance an impossibility?

The revisionist narrative is all a blur.

Colonial Masters

Your languid frame is a walking corpse.
The pent-up anger is a bubble of steaming water.
Rage and fury spread like a rising fountain.

Our colonial masters are not resting in their graves.
Their heavenly sojourn has been tainted
and watermarked by their sullied record.

The venom of hate stings like snake fangs.
These blame games have taken more than a few prisoners.
Our unending woes have blurred our memory lines.

Creative God

My mind births poetic pieces out of strange occurrences.
The fire burning in my belly and the voice in my head
are in a battle of wits.

I'm a voice of reason whose oil flows in and out of season.

With words that quake like tremor and pricks even the coldest of hearts,
my ingenuity peaks at odd hours.

My inventiveness is timeless, with vivid footprints
etched on the sands of time.

Blurred

Culture is standing on one leg.
Identity has suffered a mishap.
Our father figures have been stung by *woke* culture.
History tastes like spoilt beans.

Greener pastures are eating at the heart of our past;
Our values have become lost artifacts,

Prisoners of the west, now like the rest.
This hazy cloud is a sorry sight.

City of Lost Memories

I grew up in a city of inequalities and unfairness,
where cries of agony prick heaven's ears.
The people's saviours are in the gulag of the voiceless.
Unchained dogs carry the banner aloft, serving sorrow
for breakfast.

My left hand has no fingers.
Man's heart is a landmine.

In this city of lost memories,
Our good deeds have been wiped by hollow mist.

Entitled Uncle

There was a ringing slap on my face
That left invisible scars and marks.

My waning years have been muddled in dirt
And muddy waters.

This song of remembrance is a talking drum
escaping in the Wide.

Invisible darts are hitting the right spots.
Petulant children are in a fit of rage.

This remembrance song leaves a sour
feeling.

At the Table

I no longer bring my children to the table to eat and feast.
An overfed child once poked me in the eye.

A one-eyed man would always stand for an eye for an eye.

I'm running scared from the vengeful at heart:
Yesterday's pampered strangers have set hearts on fire,

Burning memories.

Like Judas Iscariot, the betrayal crushes the soul.

Never Ever!

Never forget the blast from the past, with remembrance that breeds hurt
and left our beautiful city in the abyss of ruins.

Never ever!

Never forget the terrorists who took our cherished memories
and left us in a dark hole.

Never ever!

Never forget bandits and terrorist sympathisers who glossed over our pain
And, through inactions and eerie silence, spoke volumes.

Never ever!

Never trivialise our collective history
as fake stories.

Never ever!

Never gloss over terror as an error of judgement.
This ideological quest, like sprouting roots, can't be erased
with a mere 'go and sin no more.'

Never ever!

Never forget the selective amnesia and
injustice that pervaded
our landscapes, and the oppressors
who rained terror with brute force.

Never ever!

On Loss

There are days I forget the synonyms of grief.
The void, memories, and silent tears cannot be wrapped
in lucid language.

There are no soothing metaphors to paint the feeling of loss
and numb the pain.

Is there a perfect way to grieve?

There are memories that crush the soul,
Like the World Trade Center turning to flames
with hollow cries staining the dark skies.

I do not understand the language of the dead; of loss and pain.

Life after death is an unravelled puzzle.

Serenade in this melody of pain; cry tears that overflow like a river
running its banks; grieve as a remembrance;

for this loss hangs like an albatross that will take an age to blur.

Needy

I have mentored people with insatiable wants who, in the real sense,
don't give a f**k.

Being an Angel to many people who needed a lifeline,

Being burdened with baggage that weighs me down,
Hypocrites and hypocrisy stood gallant, like battle-ready soldiers.

Through unfettered wisdom, I know blood is not all about family
ties.
I have learnt that good deeds can be blurred and repaid with evil.

I have learnt the language of the deaf, and have seen through the eyes of the blind.

I have learnt the art of silence and being clothed with a measure of dignity.

I have been stripped naked by lovers and wounded by familiar foes.

I have lost all
Before I could stand tall.

I have been sapped of strength by the needy,

And there is no more strength left in me.

Addiction

These accumulators accumulate debt
like an ascending stairway with no end

Gambling is eating at the soul of society. Our youngsters
are addicted to quick wins.
They fetch water in baskets.
My next-door neighbour has become a shadow.
His hopes of a big break have become a fatal illusion.

These addictions have wrecked more than a few lives.
The odds of a loss shine through with every punt.

This gambling dungeon has sent many on a downward spiral.

Who will call these untamed beasts,
wrecking lives, to order?

Fizzling

The morning dew is a ray of hope.
The sun shining is a good omen.
Life was a song
And we were smitten like lovestruck puppies.

Youthful vigour's burning has become ashes.
Life's tapestry has run its full course.

The end of this chapter is a summation of fizzling memories.

Author's Note

Thank you for the time you have taken to read this book. I hope you enjoyed the poems in it.

If you loved the book and have a minute to spare, I would appreciate a short review on the page or site where you bought it. I greatly appreciate your help in promoting my work. Reviews from readers like you make a huge difference in helping new readers choose a book.

Thank you!
Tolu' A. Akinyemi

Author's Bio

Tolu' A. Akinyemi (also known as Tolutoludo & the Lion of Newcastle) is a multi-award-winning author in the genre of poetry, short stories, children's literature, and essays. His works include Dead Lions Don't Roar (poetry, 2017); Unravel Your Hidden Gems (essays, 2018); Dead Dogs Don't Bark (poetry, 2018); Dead Cats Don't Meow (poetry, 2019); Never Play Games With the Devil (poetry, 2019); Inferno of Silence (short stories, 2020); A Booktiful Love (poetry, 2020); Black ≠ Inferior (poetry, 2021); Never Marry a Writer (poetry, 2021); Everybody Don Kolomental (poetry, 2021); I Wear Self-Confidence Like a Second Skin (children's literature, 2021); I Am Not a Troublemaker (children's literature, 2021); Born in Lockdown (poetry, 2021); A god in a Human Body (poetry, 2022); If You Have To Be Anything, Be Kind (children's literature, 2022); City of Lost Memories, (poetry, 2022); Awaken Your Inner Lion, (essays, forthcoming – September 2022); You Need More Than Dreams (poetry, forthcoming – January 2023); and The Morning Cloud is Empty (poetry, forthcoming – March 2023).

Tolu' has been endorsed by the Arts Council England as a writer of "exceptional talent."

A former headline act at Great Northern Slam, Havering Literary Festival, Crossing The Tyne Festival, and Feltonbury Arts and Music Festival, he also inspires large audiences through spoken word performances and has appeared as a keynote speaker in major forums and events. He facilitates creative writing master classes for many audiences.

His poems have appeared (or are forthcoming) in the 57th issue (Volume 15, No. 1) of the Wilderness House Literary Review; The Writers Cafe Magazine Issue 18; GN Books; Lion and Lilac; Agape Review; Continue the Voice; My Woven Poetry; Black Moon Magazine; Calla Press; and elsewhere.

His books are based on a deep reality and often reflect relationships and life, featuring people he has met in his journey as a writer. His books have inspired many people to improve their performance and/or their circumstances. Tolu' has taken his poetry to the stage, performing his written word at many events. Through his writing and these performances, he supports business leaders, other aspiring authors, and people of all ages who are interested in reading and writing. Sales of the books have allowed Tolu' donate to charity, allowing him to make a difference where he feels it's important and showing that he lives by the words he puts to page.

He is a co-founder of Lion and Lilac, a UK-based arts organisation, and sits on the board of many organisations.
Tolu' is a financial crime consultant as well as a Certified Anti-Money Laundering Specialist

(CAMS) with extensive experience working with leading investment banks and consultancy firms.

He is a trained economist from Ekiti State University (formerly known as University of Ado-Ekiti (UNAD)).

He sat for his master's degree in Accounting and Financial Management at the University of Hertfordshire, Hatfield, United Kingdom.

Tolu' was a student ambassador at the University of Hertfordshire, Hatfield, representing the university in major forums and engaging with young people during various assignments.

Tolu' Akinyemi was born in Ado-Ekiti, Nigeria and lives in the United Kingdom. Tolu' is an ardent supporter of Chelsea Football Club in London.

You can connect with Tolu' on his various social media accounts:

Instagram: @ToluToludo
Facebook: facebook.com/toluaakinyemi
   Twitter: @ToluAkinyemi

City of Lost Memories

Multi-Award-Winning Books by Tolu' A. Akinyemi
(Lion of Newcastle)

www.ingramcontent.com/pod-product-compliance
Lightning Source LLC
Chambersburg PA
CBHW030311100526
44590CB00012B/595